LUDWIG VAN BEETHOVEN

A Life From Beginning to End

Table of Contents

Introduction

Some of the music fans of Ludwig van Beethoven's day were hesitant to be introduced to him. Would the masterful composer be in an impatient mood? Were the stories about his deafness and eccentricities true? Would he even permit them to become acquainted with him? Most found Beethoven to be much more cheerful, kind, and ready for friendship than rumor had whispered. They went away with anecdotes to treasure—they had met the great musician in person; they had come into contact with a legend.

Those seeking to be introduced to Ludwig van Beethoven today meet with a volume of information. They find that Beethoven is characterized as having been one of the greatest composers in the history of western music. Music theorists explain that the emotional brilliance of Beethoven's compositions lifted music from the Classical style into the Romantic era. Beethoven's symphonies dramatically influenced the composers who came after him. His vision of music changed how musicians and listeners alike approached the way music should be composed, performed, understood, and enjoyed.

But the best way to be introduced to Ludwig van Beethoven today is still the same as it was in the days when he moved from one lodging-house to another in the city of Vienna: find someplace where his immortal *Symphony No. 9* is being performed by a full orchestra and choir and settle into a seat. As the master wrote on one of his wonderful compositions: discover that his music was "From the heart—may it return to the heart."

Chapter One

Groomed for Greatness

"Music comes to me more readily than words."

—Ludwig van Beethoven

"The baptismal certificate does not seem right," complained Ludwig van Beethoven. The document stated that the child who had been born to Johann van Beethoven and his wife Maria Magdelena had been baptized on December 17, 1770. Ludwig's grandfather, after whom he was named, was a skilled professional singer and musician. When Ludwig also showed promise of musical genius, his father Johann hurried to put his young son's talent on public display. It seems likely that Johann introduced little Ludwig as being a year or two younger than he actually was, hoping to establish him as a child prodigy like the popular Mozart. As a result, the little boy himself became confused about his true age.

Furthermore, Ludwig van Beethoven was the second child in the Beethoven family to bear his name. A brother had been given the same name a couple of years earlier, but the baby had lived for only six days. Confused about his actual birthdate, Ludwig assumed that the certificate still on record at his birthplace in Bonn, Germany, referred to his deceased older brother. Various other

[handwritten margin notes: "named after his grandpa – singer + musician"; "lied about his age so he can be perceived as great"]

preserved documents and recorded opinions about Ludwig's age and birthdate also disagree with one another. Historians have generally come to think that Ludwig was indeed born in 1770, on December 16, one day before the infant's baptismal certificate was issued.

The Beethoven family was not wealthy. When Ludwig's grandfather died in 1773, his father hoped to step into his shoes and earn a living by singing. Unfortunately, Johann struggled with alcoholism and did not share the level of talent nor the persevering industry of his father. Instead, Johann began to train his small son Ludwig at the clavier, a piano-like instrument. Years later, neighbors would remember seeing little Ludwig standing on a footstool to practice, sometimes crying at his required studies.

While he was still young, Ludwig became accomplished enough to play at court. On March 26, 1778, 8yrs he performed on the clavier for a concert along with another one of his father's music students. In the meanwhile, Ludwig received only a rudimentary public education. Further learning was all set aside to make time for his rigorous musical training. Ludwig's boyhood was perhaps lonely since he spent his time practicing the clavier and composing elaborate music while other boys studied and played together. What he enjoyed most was improvising tunes as he played, a practice which his father despised. "What silly trash are you scratching together now?" He once demanded. "You know I can't bear that—scratch by note, otherwise your scratching won't amount to much."

Soon Ludwig had come to the end of what his father could teach him. Various musicians consented here and there to give the young boy lessons, but in 1781, Ludwig officially became the pupil of Christian Gottlob Neefe, the new court organist. This relationship opened up Ludwig's first great responsibility in 1782, when Neefe temporarily ~2 yrs traveled elsewhere, leaving his duties as organist for religious services to Ludwig. The boy had to play twice every day for the Catholic masses in addition to other special services.

In 1783, the busy Neefe also asked Ludwig to take his place in playing the harpsichord (another instrument similar to a piano) for rehearsals of the court orchestra. Neefe had stretched Ludwig's capabilities by requiring him to practice the works of Johann Sebastian Bach. Now Ludwig would have to read and play a variety of complicated musical pieces, further expanding his musical education. In addition, Beethoven began producing noteworthy compositions of his own.

It was not until 1784, however, that Ludwig was officially appointed as Neefe's assistant as court organist and finally began receiving a small salary. At last, he could help to financially support his family with his music, the purpose toward which his father had groomed him practically from babyhood.

In 1787, at 16 years of age, Beethoven was sent to Vienna, Austria, to study under the musical master, Amadeus Wolfgang Mozart. It is not known whether he was able to receive lessons from Mozart, though some say that he was instructed by him in musical composition.

Unfortunately, Beethoven's mother became seriously ill with tuberculosis, and he had to hurry home from Vienna to say goodbye before her death at 40 years of age. "She was such a kind, loving mother to me, and my best friend," he mourned. "Ah, who was happier than I when I could still utter the sweet name, mother, and it was heard? And to whom can I now speak it?"

Left alone to support his increasingly alcoholic father and two younger brothers, Beethoven found a job as a music instructor with the wealthy and cultured von Breuning family. Happier days ensued as Beethoven was accepted as one of the family, even accompanying them on vacations. While he provided musical entertainment as well as instruction for his new friends, they introduced him to the interactions of a happy, healthy family and a supportive environment. Beethoven experienced several romantic crushes toward pretty young lady friends of the family. He made friends with young Count Ferdinand von Waldstein, who would significantly foster Beethoven's musical success. And he continued to play in the orchestra and compose his own music.

In 1792, Beethoven was again able to travel to Vienna for further musical education. Mozart had died, but the famous Joseph Haydn could be engaged as his instructor. Beethoven made the journey from Bonn to Vienna in a post-chaise. His boyhood in Bonn had come to an end.

Chapter Two

Star on the Rise

"Music should strike fire from the heart of man and bring tears from the eyes of woman."

—Ludwig van Beethoven

Beethoven's need to move reputably in the social scenes of Vienna incurred him many additional expenses. In his new budget, he listed not only living expenditures but also the costs of new, more expensive clothing and even dancing lessons. While he was still occupied with the task of settling in, Beethoven received news that his father had died on December 18, 1792. Now he was fully responsible for the financial support of his younger brothers. His boyhood was indeed behind him.

At first, Beethoven found his new teacher, Joseph Haydn, to be somewhat too occupied with his current work in musical composition to provide the systematic instruction that Beethoven knew he needed. Although Beethoven could already read and play complex music with ease and improvise beautiful harmonies with dramatic flair, he struggled with Haydn's preliminary lessons on what was considered to be correct counterpoint composition (music with two or more independent melodic lines). Finally, he agreed to receive secret instruction from Johann Schenk, an accomplished musician and composer who took an interest in Beethoven after hearing how he could play. Schenk introduced Beethoven to the basic rules of counterpoint composition. For a time, he even helped to correct his exercises before they were returned to his official instructor, Haydn.

In January 1794, Haydn left for London, and Beethoven continued his studies in strict counterpoint composition with Johann Albrechtsberger. It is also thought possible that he received lessons in vocal composition from Antonio Salieri and violin lessons from Ignaz Schuppanzigh during this time as well. Already confident in his abilities and often impatient, impulsive, and stubborn in nature, Beethoven had to discipline himself to submit to the instruction of others and to the tedious effort of completing musical exercises according to established, rigid rules. But slowly, his compositions began to exhibit the results of his efforts. Beethoven's music improved. He was able to take the structures which he was being taught and weave his distinctive style through them.

Meanwhile, the musical culture of Vienna at this point revolved around personal salons at which Beethoven became extremely popular. His gifted piano improvisations coupled with his ability to perform music by Bach or, for that matter, instantly read and play any of the complicated music of the day made him friends among wealthy and influential people. Soon, Beethoven was living as a guest of one of his friends, Prince Karl

Lichnowsky, and had enough extra funds to enable him to support a personal servant and even keep a horse of his own for riding.

On March 29, 1795, Beethoven made his first appearance at a public concert in Vienna. The concert, organized by Antonio Salieri for the benefit of widows and orphans, featured only two musicians. Antonio Cartellieri, the first young musician, performed an oratorio. Beethoven composed an original concerto and played it on the pianoforte along with orchestral accompaniment. The very next day, Beethoven appeared in a second concert, where he improvised on the piano and played a piece by Mozart. At last, the general public was able to enjoy his music, which had formerly been performed only in private gatherings.

Following these successes, Beethoven published a series of three piano trios as Opus 1. The pieces not only gained Beethoven further fame, but they contributed significantly to Beethoven's financial means as well.

On November 22, 1795, a highly publicized dance was held for which Beethoven composed the musical arrangements. On December 18 of the same year, he played one of his original compositions and three symphonies by Haydn for yet another successful concert. Beethoven's star was on the rise. That year, his two younger brothers joined him in making their livings in Vienna. Beethoven was able to recommend pupils to the older of the brothers, Carl Casper, who became a successful music teacher. Ludwig also offered financial support to the younger brother, Johann, who was eventually able to establish a business as an apothecary.

For so long, the law has been used to weaponize those that are most vulnerable to societal flaws, as a constitutional lawyer it is my mission to ~~the~~ law transform the meaning and interpretation of law to ensure it is used as a vessel of freedom for our rights; but also administered in a fair & just manner. I believe y'all can provide an learning environment that will allow me to understand the law on a deeper level

Chapter Three

Mood Swings and Love Interests

"I wish you music to help with the burdens of life and to ❤
help you release your happiness to others."

—Ludwig van Beethoven

In 1796, Beethoven traveled to Prague with Prince Lichnowsky and found his music so well received that he continued traveling, making a tour that included Berlin, where he played for King William Frederick II. It is thought that he may even have received but declined an invitation from the king to become a professional musician in his court in Prussia. It is certain that he made friends with Friedrich Heinrich Himmel, the famous pianist of King Fredrick's court, with whom he would correspond by letters afterward.

On June 21, Beethoven attended a meeting of the Berliner Singakademie, a prestigious musical society. Beethoven listened to the choir's singing with enjoyment and then concluded the session with a piano improvisation of his own. Afterward, the audience gathered around him, weeping with the emotion his performance had inspired. Beethoven, on the other hand, often followed his most satisfactory piano improvisations by breaking into loud laughter. Now, instead of appreciating the crowd's deeply emotional response, he complained that they had not clapped for him.

By November 1796, Beethoven had finished his tour and was back in Vienna, where he settled down to composing and publishing sonatas for the violoncello and pianoforte. The new year of 1797 found him teaching a full slate of music pupils, performing at concerts, publishing new compositions, and flourishing financially and socially. One of the most popular compositions published during this time was Beethoven's *Adelaide,* a song for solo voice and piano that Beethoven had composed and published in part as long ago as 1795. Now he finally finished the song, which accompanied the words to a romantic poem by Friedrich von Matthisson.

In 1798, competition to Beethoven's genius arrived in Vienna in the form of another master of the pianoforte, Joseph Wölfl of Salzburg. Wölfl had studied under Leopold Mozart (the father of Wolfgang Amadeus Mozart) and Michael Haydn (the younger brother of Joseph Haydn) and had been making his way in Warsaw as an acclaimed pianoforte teacher and composer.

Wölfl's finesse prompted Beethoven to practice and perfect his own techniques on the pianoforte. Although Beethoven's dramatic improvisations were generally considered to be more skillful than Wölfl's, Beethoven was admittedly sometimes lacking in precision in his performances. Soon, the two could be found engaging in friendly piano duels at the beautiful villa of Baron

Raymond von Wetzlar, each improvising in turn to the delight of their listening audience.

Wölfl had extraordinarily large hands, which enabled him to perform wonders on the keys of the pianoforte. Nothing could match the passion of Beethoven's playing, however, ranging from the pensive to the ethereal, the stormy to the tranquil, sometimes all in a single performance. In fact, Beethoven occasionally received criticism from his more educated listeners for what was considered his extreme originality. They complained that the musical train of thought of his compositions was often rudely interrupted by his sudden flights of melodic fantasy.

A violinist named Karl Amenda arrived in Vienna about this time and became Beethoven's nearly inseparable companion due to their mutual enjoyment of each other's music. Amenda later related that when he once deplored the fact that Beethoven's marvelous improvisations were "born and lost in a moment," Beethoven refuted this statement by accurately replaying every note of the impromptu piece he had just completed.

Another time, Amenda happened to be on hand when Beethoven came up short on cash when his rent was due. Amenda told Beethoven that he didn't have a problem; boldly, he locked Beethoven into his room, gave him an assignment, and returned after three hours had passed. Beethoven shoved over a paper on which a new musical composition was written. Amenda took the paper to Beethoven's landlord and instructed him to take it to a publisher and collect the rent that was due to him. The

[handwritten margin notes: "Beethoven was often forgetful ADHD"; "Sounds a lil cocky"]

landlord was dubious, but he returned from the publisher asking if "other bits of paper like that were to be had."

In 1799, Beethoven was engaged to give piano lessons to the wealthy and aristocratic von Brunswick daughters, Therese and Josephine. Beethoven, always susceptible to sudden romantic crushes, was deeply attracted to 20-year-old Josephine. Her family, however, soon arranged a socially and financially advantageous marriage for her with another man, Count Joseph Deym. Nonetheless, Beethoven continued to visit the Deym home and instruct Josephine on the piano as the years went by and she bore four children to her husband.

Many of Beethoven's relationships followed a rocky path. In fact, it was common for him to become estranged from many of his companions following bitter arguments that often could be traced back to rash words or actions on his part. Naturally impulsive and strong-willed, pushed into a heady society at a young age, Beethoven had never received the type of wise, consistent guidance from his father that would have helped him learn to control his emotions. Even as an adult, Beethoven could be furiously angry one moment and pitifully repentant the next. Although he often showed evidence of sincere humility, Beethoven had been primed to expect fame and favor from the time he was a small child, and his pride had swelled as a result. Once he even commented that he valued certain friends "only by what they do for me." He declared, "I look upon them only as instruments upon which I play when I feel so disposed."

Varying in mood from sensitive and kindly to infuriated and petulant, Beethoven was hiding an unhappy secret, one that he dared not admit even to himself; it was becoming difficult for him to hear.

Chapter Four

Beethoven's Deafness and Depression

"Music is like a dream. One that I cannot hear."

—Ludwig van Beethoven

Beethoven's Symphony No. 1 in C Major was first publicly performed at the Royal Imperial Theater on April 2, 1800. It was a triumph for Beethoven, demonstrating his increasing mastery of his musical talents. On March 28, 1801, his only full-length ballet was premiered, *The Creatures of Prometheus*. Beethoven also completed one of his most famous and enchanting pieces during this year, his Piano Sonata No. 14, which would come to be known and loved as the *Moonlight Sonata*.

Even as his compositions grew in power and fame, however, Beethoven himself sank into a black depression. Despite seeing a succession of doctors and attempting a multitude of prescribed remedies, including various baths, herbs, and oils, Beethoven suffered from debilitating, chronic diarrhea and general ill-health. And no matter what happened, he could never escape the ever-louder ringing in his ears.

In 1802, Beethoven retreated from Vienna to the countryside of Heiligenstadt, where he wrote what has come to be called the *Heiligenstadt Testament,* a letter to his younger brothers. The epistle began with the words, "Oh you men who think or say that I am malevolent, stubborn, or misanthropic, how greatly do you wrong me. You do not know the secret cause which makes me seem that way to you."

Beethoven went on to describe how he had expected since childhood to accomplish great things with his life but how, even before 30 years of age, his inevitable deafness was slowly becoming ever more certain. Ashamed to admit that he—the great musician who had built his entire life upon what he could hear—was no longer able to comprehend much of what people said to him, Beethoven avoided society and was often rude to those whom he could not understand. "I would have ended my life," he averred. "It was only my art that held me back. Ah, it seemed to me impossible to leave the world until I had brought forth all that I felt was within me."

Sick at his fate, Beethoven begged his brothers to give the letter to his doctor so that his condition could finally be made public after his death, hoping that the knowledge of his terrible infirmity would cause people to judge his actions and attitudes less harshly.

Although he had decided not to commit suicide, Beethoven really could not imagine life without his sense of hearing. He named his brothers as his heirs and encouraged Carl, "Recommend virtue to your children; it alone, not money, can make them happy." He bid his friends goodbye and said, "With joy I hasten towards death." In his next words, however, with typical inconsistency, Beethoven hoped that he would not die until he had developed all of his musical abilities.

Beethoven had always found inspiration in nature, taking regular walks outdoors no matter the weather, and during the period of his illness, he spent even more time in the countryside, especially during the hot summer months. He would wander the country roads, communing with nature, speaking to God in prayer, and seeking comfort for his bitter fears.

All sorts of theories were constructed both during Beethoven's life and afterward as to the origins of his deafness, from possible nerve injury to arterial disease to potential typhus. The true cause was never discovered— and neither was a cure. As all music faded gradually from Beethoven's hearing, he resolved to devote his talents to composition. Although eventually he would no longer be able to improvise on the piano for social functions, he would always be able to hear new and splendid musical compositions ringing within his mind. He would still be able to transfer these compositions to paper as he had been trained.

Beethoven's ambitions flamed into a fierce passion. He began to wake early enough to compose for two hours even before his breakfast. Always somewhat untidy in his personal habits, Beethoven allowed his rooms to become littered with scraps of crumpled and discarded compositions which the maid was forbidden to clear away just in case he should ever wish to consult them again. Unfinished manuscripts mingled with the deteriorating remains of unfinished lunches, carelessly stacked books, and a litter of odds and ends. Even the chamber pot kept underneath his piano sometimes went unemptied.

When he visited a restaurant, Beethoven was likely to become distracted for hours, scribbling notes on the menu. He might even absentmindedly eat and leave without paying his bill—or pay and leave without eating at all.

As his musical compositions improved and multiplied, Beethoven's mental and physical health improved as well. He began to associate with his friends again. Ultimately, he would have to accept public knowledge of his loss of hearing. In the meanwhile, Beethoven composed.

Chapter Five

Melodies of the Soul

*"What I have in my heart and soul must find a way out.
That's the reason for music."*

—Ludwig van Beethoven

Austrian newspapers announced that the Theater-an-der-Wien would host the performance of Beethoven's very first oratorio, *Christ on the Mount of* Olives, on April 5, 1803, along with his Symphony No. 2. Realizing that with the exception of Joseph Haydn's, his own name was probably already known as that of the world's most talented living composer, Beethoven had confidence that this first vocal composition of his own would be a profitable attraction. Accordingly, he doubled the cost of the regular places in the theater and raised the prices of the best seats even higher.

Five o'clock on the morning of the concert found Beethoven sitting in bed, jotting down changes in the score for the trombone section of the orchestra. The final rehearsal began three hours later. By mid-afternoon everyone was tired and frustrated, and the arrival of big baskets containing lunch foods and wine contributed by Prince Lichnowsky were gladly accepted. The rehearsal went on.

That night at the performance, Beethoven asked the musical director of the theater to turn the pages of his notebook for him as he played at the piano. To the director's dismay, he discovered that aside from some indecipherably scribbled notes, much of Beethoven's notebook was blank—how would he ever know when to turn the pages at the correct time? Beethoven, recognizing his friend's distress, was amused. With a twinkle in his eye, he gave a slight signal whenever he was ready for a page to be turned. Other than the few notations he had made for himself, he was able to play the piece from memory until he could find the leisure to write it down.

The oratorio was enough of a success to be replayed in the theater for years, always with a full house, although not even Beethoven himself considered it one of his best works. Nonetheless, it was an important branching out of his skills.

In spite of his encroaching deafness, Beethoven's fame was still on the rise. A number of portraits had already been painted of him. About this time, a full-length oil painting was made by the musical enthusiast Joseph Mähler. Beethoven's stocky frame, broad hands, wild, dark hair, and pock-marked, somber face appeared against a classical background, seated with a hand resting on the lyre guitar before him.

Beethoven had always treasured a portrait of his musically talented grandfather Ludwig, carrying it first of all into every new living quarters and finding a place of honor in which to display it. The grandfather's portrait, painted with the elaborate symbolism characteristic of the times, had depicted a dark cape falling from his shoulders to the ground, most likely demonstrating that he was recovering from the sadness of the death of his wife. Beethoven's own portrait likewise shows a crumpled cape lying in the dark shadows behind his chair as he turns toward the light before him; he would put his despair over his loss of hearing in the background and embrace the possibilities that remained.

Now the completion of his Symphony No. 3 occupied Beethoven's attention. He had already written the title on the cover page of his copy of the score; the symphony would honor Napoleon Bonaparte, hero of the French Revolution. In Beethoven's mind, Bonaparte stood for equality and democracy. Too often, even when artists of Beethoven's day were celebrated and universally welcomed into the highest of echelons of society, they were nonetheless considered to be on an unequal footing with their aristocratic benefactors. For instance, marriage between one of the ladies of the aristocratic class and the brilliant, famous Beethoven would have been considered inappropriate.

Napoleon Bonaparte, on the other hand, was thought to be an inspiring champion of true equality for the middle class. Some of Beethoven's friends were with him when the news arrived from Paris. Bonaparte, the hope of democracy, had crowned himself emperor of France. "Is then he, too, nothing more than an ordinary human being?" Beethoven cried out. "Now he, too, will trample on all the rights of man and indulge only his ambition." Some reported that Beethoven tore the title page in half and threw it to the floor. Others said that he scratched Bonaparte's name out so deeply that he left a hole in the paper where it had been. In fact, a copy matching this description still exists on display in Vienna today.

In any case, Symphony No. 3 would be performed for private audiences in the spring of 1804 as the *Sinfonia Eroica* (the Heroic Symphony). Only the aspiring nature of the piece itself would reflect Beethoven's visions of a boundary-conquering genius.

Beethoven continued to regularly visit his former student Josephine, now the Countess Deym, whose husband had recently died of pneumonia. The couple's love for one another grew as they exchanged a series of tender love letters in which Beethoven passionately addressed Josephine as his only beloved, his everything, and his supreme joy. Nonetheless, the two kept their feelings a strict secret, probably because Josephine's family would have rejected Beethoven as a suitor since he belonged to a lower social class than their own. Josephine may even have feared that she would lose guardianship of the four small children she had borne to the now-deceased count if she formed a marriage alliance with Beethoven.

Sunday afternoon, April 7, 1805, Symphony No. 3 was publicly performed at the same theater where Beethoven had successfully aired his first oratorio. Nearly an hour in length, it was a much longer symphony than had been presented to audiences before. In fact, someone in the crowd finally shouted out, "I'll give another [dollar] if the thing will but stop!"

After the performance, critics accused Beethoven of sacrificing all thematic continuity and even audience enjoyment in the symphony for the sake of displaying his powers of originality in composition. The musicians themselves found the symphony difficult to interpret and perform. "A certain undesirable originality may be achieved without much trouble," one magazine correspondent scoffed. "But genius proclaims itself not in the unusual and the fantastic, but in the beautiful and the sublime."

In spite of public criticism, Symphony No. 3 came to be recognized as a turning point in music, a masterfully constructed challenge to the accepted nature of music itself.

Beethoven showed unmasked irritation at the lack of hearty applause from the audience, shrugged his shoulders at the critics, and turned his attention to his first and only opera, the *Fidelio* (or *Leonore*) to be publicly performed in the theater on November 20, 1805, and his Symphony No. 4, which would appear in private concert in March 1807.

Chapter Six

Passion for Music

"I despise a world which does not feel that music is a higher revelation than all wisdom and philosophy."

—Ludwig van Beethoven

Beethoven's continued struggle with his ever-escalating loss of hearing increased not only his fervor of composition but his personal peculiarities as well. Often his displays of temper were downright violent, engendering such undignified scenes as one in which he flung a plate of food at the head of a waiter who had brought him the wrong order. Likely as not, the incident probably ended with an especially large tip, which was Beethoven's typical resolution for his frequent altercations with restaurant staff. Although he was well-known for quarreling with his closest friends and even with his two younger brothers, Beethoven was also quick to take blame and seek reconciliation in the humblest of terms.

His extreme spectrums of moodiness led those who knew Beethoven to describe him in widely varying ways. Sometimes musicians who played in the orchestra for his concerts would note his good-hearted patience, remembering how he would laugh as if it were a pleasant joke when the difficulties of his complex and surprising compositions caused them to break down in rehearsal, encouraging them that they would get it right the next time around. In contrast, he was once guilty of accusing an entire orchestra of deliberately ruining his music when they did not play it in the spirit in which he had intended. At a later time, the musicians of one orchestra actually refused to rehearse as long as Beethoven were present.

It was certainly not uncommon for people to characterize Beethoven as being exceptionally-rude—to audiences who did not respond as he desired, to musicians whose talent he either envied or did not admire, to friends or even strangers who provoked him—to anyone. Those who loved him and trusted his basic good nature chose to construe much of his rudeness as a form of blunt honesty and dislike for flattery. Feeling that he deserved special treatment because of his artistic talent and temperament, Beethoven did not discipline himself to control his excesses of emotion or conform to good manners—and usually his expectation of special treatment was not disappointed. Friends and family forgave him, fans indulged him as an eccentric musical genius, and history would excuse him on the basis of his desperate battle with hearing loss.

A characteristic example occurred when Beethoven was associated with Archduke Rudolph. Beethoven's social blunders were so persistent that at last the archduke laughingly decreed that Beethoven would simply not be held subject to the usual laws of court etiquette.

When at social gatherings, Beethoven often refused to play on the piano for the entertainment of his friends unless he was very persistently coaxed. Once he had complied, he would then become furious if anyone disrupted the music by chatting in the background or providing any type of distraction. Upon occasion, he threatened to never play for certain individuals again who had happened to displease him, and with characteristic stubbornness, he kept his word.

Beethoven had an even deeper, almost paranoid aversion to anyone's chancing to hear him as he improvised on the piano in private. Understandably, he would also often become enraged if he were disrupted in the process of composing a new work.

In his habits, Beethoven was a naturally clumsy person. He frequently dropped things, knocked objects over, or crashed into the furniture. Even his handwriting was a discouraging scrawl. Perhaps this was due in part to the fact that the childhood smallpox which had badly pitted his face had also left him with rather poor eyesight. When he was performing at the piano, however, Beethoven was all grace. His hands themselves seemed hardly to move as his fingers rippled over the keys, his body bent slightly forward over the instrument, his face calm and impassive.

He was not so stoic when conducting an orchestra on a piece of his own composition. Striving with every fiber to communicate the spirit of the music to the musicians, Beethoven would bodily crouch lower and lower whenever the song became softer, then spring into the air with widely gesticulating arms whenever the volume suddenly increased. Caught up in his inner world of song, Beethoven yielded less and less to the social pressures that surrounded him. Nothing mattered to him in comparison with his passion for music.

Chapter Seven

Für Elise

"Music is the mediator between the spiritual and the sensual life."

—Ludwig van Beethoven

Beethoven's quick temper, characteristically rude remarks, and difficult attitudes complicated his first public production of his famous Symphony No. 5 and the lesser-known Symphony No. 6 in December of 1808. Unable to get along with the members of the orchestra and having driven a soloist away by his abrasive behavior, Beethoven struggled through the single, fractured rehearsal that was held during the morning.

That evening, other factors also contributed negatively to the performance. The planned program of several lengthy songs was extended enough to weary even an avid audience. Furthermore, the theater was miserably chilly. Special directions had been given for a change in the music of Symphony No. 5, but after only one rehearsal under strained conditions, it was easy to forget. Predictably, when that place in the score was reached, some of the musicians began playing at the wrong time. Discord resulted. Frustrated, Beethoven stopped the orchestra entirely, directed them where to begin again, and had them play the part a second time, much to the embarrassment of the musicians.

Such events drove Beethoven to develop a growing sense of deliberate persecution and neglect. As his failing hearing sometimes prohibited him from correctly understanding everything that was going on about him, he became increasingly suspicious of the intents of his friends and fellow musicians.

In 1809, Beethoven was offered a permanent place as a musician in the court of Napoleon Bonaparte. Hurt by the growing difficulties in his relationships with the people about him, Beethoven seriously considered accepting the offer. His aristocratic friends, however, were alarmed at the potential loss of their musical genius. Soon they had drafted a binding agreement to financially maintain Beethoven as long as he would continue to compose and live in Vienna. Beethoven had always struggled with his finances, often managing them unwisely and having no consistent means of support. He decided to accept the agreement.

A characteristic example of the frequent misunderstandings that arose between Beethoven and his friends quickly followed. Ferdinand Ries, Beethoven's student, secretary, and close friend for the last eight years, was advised to try to get the position that had been rejected by Beethoven for himself in the hopes that he might be engaged at even half the wages that had been offered to Beethoven. Ries instantly attempted to go to Beethoven for counsel. Beethoven, however, jumped to the conclusion that Ries had been attempting to snatch the proffered court position away from him and refused even to see his friend or answer his letters for three weeks. When Ries did manage to come into contact with Beethoven, he sneered, "So—do you think that you can fill a position which was offered to me?"

Realizing that the opportunity to get the appointment would soon pass, Ries went to Beethoven's house the next morning and ended up throwing a servant to the floor in his determination to gain entrance to the room where Beethoven was playing the piano. When Beethoven came out to investigate the disturbance and at last agreed to listen to his friend, he realized and fully admitted that he had misjudged Ries' intentions. Instantly, he went with Ries to try to help him gain the appointment, but it was too late.

Beethoven may have been nursing a private heartache beyond the gradual loss of his hearing. Correspondence from this period of his life strongly hints of hopes of marriage, but no marriage took place. Beethoven's last preserved letter to his secret flame, Countess Josephine Deym, had ended with the words, "You want me to tell you how I am. A more difficult question could not be put to me, and I prefer to leave it unanswered, rather than to answer it too truthfully. Farewell, dear J., as always, your eternally devoted Beethoven." In February 1810, Josephine began an unhappy marriage with a baron named Christoph von Stackelberg, to whom she had already birthed an illegitimate child.

Although he had a significant number of romantic interests throughout his life, Beethoven's pursuit of love would never bring him a wife, home, or family. An undated letter to an unknown woman whom he addressed as his "Immortal Beloved" revealed the depth of his feelings. "I have determined to wander about for so long far away, until I can fly into your arms and call myself quite at home with you, can send my soul enveloped by yours into the realm of spirits." It was in 1810 that Beethoven composed *Für Elise,* a famous piano bagatelle dedicated "for Elise," a woman whose identity is also unknown. The song was never published during his lifetime.

In spite of his emotional battles, Beethoven did not doubt his worth as a musical visionary. Once he is said to have communicated his opinions to Johann Wolfgang von Goethe, an author and poet who shared Beethoven's status as a respected artist outside the ranks of aristocracy. Beethoven reportedly told Goethe a story about how he was once made to wait for an unreasonable length of time in an antechamber before he could begin to give music lessons to a duke.

When the lesson finally began, Beethoven deliberately twisted the unfortunate duke's fingers as he showed him how to play and treated him so poorly that the duke finally demanded to know why Beethoven was so impatient. Beethoven replied that the duke had already made him waste so much of his time in waiting for the lesson to start that he could no longer afford to exhibit patience. Then Beethoven apparently stated to the duke that although aristocracy could be conferred, it did not demonstrate true worth. Beethoven is said to have exclaimed, "That which you cannot make and which you are far from being, therefore, you must learn to have respect."

Beethoven refused to accord the aristocratic class the marks of honor which were usually expected from men of his class. He did not step aside for aristocrats, dress to impress them, or address them humbly. At the same time, by reason of his talent, he considered himself above the level of the common people who labored for their living.

At home, Beethoven's burden of private sorrows was further aggravated by his continuing bouts of ill health, extensive family troubles involving his younger brothers, and ongoing financial difficulties. It was a dark time. Beethoven's monetary troubles were temporarily assuaged by a successful second repetition of a concert originally held on December 8, 1813. The first concert benefited wounded soldiers returning from defeat at the Battle of Hanau, where they had failed to prevent Napoleon Bonaparte from retreating into France. Beethoven conducted a premiere of his Symphony No. 7 at the concert, which also featured another one of his new compositions, *Wellington's Victory*.

Symphony No. 8 would be performed on February 27, 1814. Once again, Beethoven would conduct the orchestra, though by this time he had become so deaf that the musicians could not truly rely on his timing.

Chapter Eight

Guardianship of His Nephew Karl

"Music is the electrical soil in which the spirit lives, thinks, and invents."

—Ludwig van Beethoven

On November 20, 1815, Ludwig van Beethoven's brother Carl Casper died of tuberculosis, appointing his brother Ludwig as guardian of his son Karl in his will. Not yet ten years old, the little nephew was the only child of the three van Beethoven brothers. And as his father had done before him, Ludwig van Beethoven viewed the boy as a potential vessel for carrying the van Beethoven musical genius into the future.

Beethoven's first thought was to remove the lad from the influence of his mother, Johanna. Beethoven had vehemently opposed his brother's marriage to Johanna from the start, claiming that she had a bad reputation. Although Carl naturally resented this interference, Beethoven's judgment was not incorrect. The two had a miserable marriage, during which Johanna faked a burglary in her own home, accusing her maid of stealing three valuable strings of pearls which Johanna was supposed to be selling under a commission but had actually purloined for herself.

Carl's will, however, specifically stated that he did not want his son Karl to be separated from his mother. "I recommend compliance to my wife and more moderation to my brother," he had written. "God permit them to be more harmonious for the sake of my child's welfare. This is the last wish of the dying husband and brother." Disregarding his brother's dying wish, Beethoven appealed to a court of law to give him the sole guardianship of his nephew, citing his mother's immoral lifestyle as sufficient reason. On January 9, 1816, the court ruled in his favor.

In February, Beethoven enrolled the little boy in a prestigious private boarding school in Vienna, instructing the proprietor not to allow his mother to have any further influence over him. Johanna, however, continually appeared at the school or sent messengers in an attempt to kidnap her son from the establishment. This persistent aggravation led the school to join forces with Beethoven in further petitioning the court that Karl's mother be completely excluded from any contact with her son whatsoever, on the grounds that she significantly disturbed him in his studies. This project met with success. In order to ensure that the boy's education was not being hindered by his mother's visits, the court ruled that Johanna could see her son only when and where Ludwig van Beethoven permitted.

That summer, Karl underwent a surgical operation for a hernia, after which Beethoven took him home with him for a time. Beethoven would have liked to have had the boy live with him throughout the year, but he was forced to return Karl to the school by the realization that he was unable to provide an adequate home environment for his little nephew.

In May 1817, a contract was signed between Johanna and Beethoven which required the boy's mother to pay part of the expenses of Karl's education. Johanna requested that she be permitted to meet with Karl at Beethoven's house. Not wishing to appear inhumane in his handling of the situation, Beethoven acquiesced. Afterward, however, he regretted having allowed Karl to associate so freely with his mother, claiming that his nephew's attitudes were very negatively affected by Johanna's influence. He worried about the behavior and moral training of his ward, encouraging the school proprietor to make sure that the little boy was made to obey.

Of course, Ludwig van Beethoven did not neglect the musical instruction of the last of the van Beethovens. One of his students, Carl Czerny, was employed to give piano lessons to little Karl, with admonitions not to push the boy too hard.

In January 1818, Beethoven managed to make the household adjustments necessary for sharing his home with his nephew, whom he removed from the boarding school. He put Karl in a class of boys taught by a local priest, but unfortunately Karl acted as such a troublemaker that the priest yielded to the complaints of the other boys and their parents and dismissed him from the class within a month.

Habitually failing to control his own emotional excesses, Beethoven was undoubtedly unable to provide the consistent, balanced training that Karl needed. Instead, he treated the boy sometimes with undue strictness and at others with unwise leniency. Furthermore, he openly encouraged him to speak disrespectfully and hatefully about his mother Johanna, whom Beethoven had long dubbed "Queen of the Night" in reference to her immorality. Torn between natural love for his mother and an equally natural desire to please his uncle, it is not surprising that Karl was prone to misbehavior. The boy was then sent to public school, and his mother renewed the legal battle over his guardianship.

On December 3, 1818, 12-year-old Karl was caught by Beethoven in some deviltry, and possibly to escape punishment, ran away from home to his mother, leaving a note behind. Beethoven called for the assistance of the police in retrieving him, and the boy was placed back into the private boarding school which he had attended before and where the managing family was very sympathetic to Beethoven's cause.

In the meanwhile, the priest who had served as Karl's teacher gave a testimony in court against Beethoven's fitness to act as a guardian to his nephew, citing Karl's bad behavior. Johanna complained that Karl was not well cared for in his uncle's house, being allowed to go dirty and without proper clothing. In view of Karl's having attempted to run away from his uncle, the court suspended Beethoven's guardianship for a few weeks, and the boy returned to live with his mother.

By March, Beethoven had made up his mind to have Karl become the legal ward of a certain magisterial councilor, hoping by this means to separate him from his mother. The plan was not wholly successful, but Karl was sent to a new boarding school and seemed at first to be doing well as the acrimonious legal battle over his guardianship dragged on. April 8, 1820, finally saw a resolution. Ludwig van Beethoven was to remain the legal guardian of his nephew Karl.

Chapter Nine

Crescendo

"Music is the one incorporeal entrance into the higher world of knowledge which comprehends mankind but which mankind cannot comprehend."

—Ludwig van Beethoven

At 50 years old, Beethoven was too deaf to engage in conversation. At home, people communicated with him by writing on a slate or any available scrap of paper. When he left the house, he would slip one of his small notebooks, which he called conversation books, into his pockets. It was widely agreed that Beethoven remained able to tell whether or not his music was being played correctly, however, just by watching the fingers of the performing musician.

Beethoven still drew inspiration from nature and kept to his habits of a daily ramble outdoors. Once, he went so far across the countryside that he lost his way. People who observed the disheveled man wandering near their homes assumed that he was a beggar. Someone called the police, who arrested him. "I am Beethoven," Ludwig protested, but the officer was not convinced. How could this disreputably clothed, untidy fellow possibly be the great composer? Beethoven was to be kept under arrest in the watch-house until morning, but he repeatedly pleaded with the policeman in charge to call someone who could identify him. Finally, the officer complied, and of course the identity of the vagrant was indeed established as the widely celebrated Ludwig van Beethoven.

Although he could not hear the orchestra well enough now to effectively conduct his works, Beethoven was still writing music. He had at least two epic compositions and many smaller ones underway, on which he labored with incredible intensity.

Neither had Beethoven's fame diminished. Once when he returned to rent a summer cottage that he had occupied the year before, the landlord demanded that the shutters, which were missing, be replaced. Beethoven had struggled severely with his eyesight in the preceding months and was glad to agree, thinking that he would need to protect his vision from the glaring sunlight. Eventually, however, the reason for the missing shutters was revealed. One of Beethoven's idiosyncrasies included the habit of scribbling notes everywhere, including on his window shutters. After Beethoven had vacated the cottage the year before, the landlord had been able to sell all of the shutters as Ludwig van Beethoven souvenirs.

Always troubled over his finances, Beethoven had for a long time been desperately bargaining for the best possible price for his *Missa Solemnis*, a monumental choral composition for Catholic mass on which he had worked for nearly five years. First, he had promised it to one publisher, even receiving an advance of funds. Then, he had decided to promise the yet uncompleted work to several other potential publishers, creating a whirlwind of correspondence that was understandably not always pleasant in nature. Now, in 1824, the masterpiece was finally finished and ready to be performed.

In his composition of this important work in D major, Beethoven reported that he "gave it all that he was humanly and artistically capable of, with utter devotion and fervor." The entire mass would last for nearly 90 minutes and include four soloists along with the choir and an especially large orchestra. It was a crowning accomplishment to Beethoven's works.

In addition, Beethoven had composed a transcendent Ninth Symphony that would include choral voices, something that had never been done by any major composer in the past. The words were taken from Friedrich Schiller's "Ode to Joy," a mystical, worshipful celebration of joy, nature, and human brotherhood. Symphony No. 9 was also more than an hour long and throbbed with the creative passions of the master composer.

But Beethoven was reluctant to plan a public performance of the mass or the symphony in Vienna. He complained to his friends that concert audiences in Vienna no longer understood his works. Would enough people even attend the event to make it financially practical? Beethoven's friends scoffed at his fears. Someone composed an eloquent and flattering letter begging him to produce a concert that would include his new songs. Prince Lichnowsky, in whose household Beethoven had lived soon after he came to Vienna, secured 30 signatures for the letter from wealthy and influential friends.

Beethoven was touched and encouraged, but he still found it difficult to get down to the business of making the necessary arrangements for the performance. Once again, his friends conspired with one little stratagem after another to induce Beethoven to plan the concert.

At last the details were worked out, and it was time for the rehearsal. Parts of both the mass and the symphony were on the program. Things were going quite well in spite of the fact that the new compositions were difficult to perform. In fact, none of the lead singers were able to reach some of the highest notes on the score. Soloists, singers, and choirmaster joined in begging Beethoven to alter his composition, but he refused. It sounded heavenly within his mind, and he was unable to hear the fact that the vocalists left out the notes that they were unable to sing.

Beethoven's deafness created yet another problem. Who would conduct the orchestra? No one wished to bar Beethoven from directing his crowning masterpieces. However, the musicians could not possibly follow a conductor who might be directing at a place in the song several minutes ahead of or behind an orchestra that he could not hear.

On May 7, 1824, Ludwig van Beethoven conducted his most inspired works before a crowded and enthusiastic theater. The glorious music swept exultantly through his veins, rising to an irresistible crescendo that filled his throbbing being. Beethoven conducted with all his might, characteristically demonstrating the changes in volume and tempo with his whole body, even though the musicians were not following his baton. For practical purposes, another director was simultaneously employed.

The stories say that Beethoven was still directing when the Ninth Symphony was finished and the room was filled with applause. Young Caroline Unger, the lead soloist, tugged at his sleeve. Hats and handkerchiefs were waving from hands everywhere. During the concert, Beethoven had been given five standing ovations.

Chapter Ten

Karl's Suicide Attempt and Beethoven's Final Notes

"I live wholly in my music."

—Ludwig van Beethoven

In 1825, Beethoven entered his 19-year-old nephew Karl in the Polytechnic Institute. Although intelligent and capable, Karl was not an industrious student. He wanted to enter the army, but such a career was abhorrent to Beethoven, who had much higher dreams for the last of the van Beethovens.

At first, with the advantage of his natural abilities, Karl did well in the Institute. Unfortunately, the good reports did not last. His studies were soon abandoned for drinking, gambling, and pursuing prostitutes. Of course, Beethoven tried to set the young man straight, but Karl had long become accustomed to his uncle's bouts of angry austerity and knew how to soothe and flatter him into doting indulgence again.

Beethoven's friends gave advice. One of the younger men offered to try to befriend Karl so that he could go about with him, hopefully curb his excesses, and introduce him to better entertainments and society.

Beethoven was unimpressed with these ideas. He felt that Karl deserved to be punished for his behavior like a disobedient child. He ordered that Karl not be permitted to go out at night without his own written permission. He made himself sick and depressed by hounding the young man, waiting to walk him home from school, worrying about the path he was choosing for himself in life.

Characteristically, he alternated between pleading pitifully with his nephew—writing, "Do not make me fear. Oh, think of my sufferings!"—and at another time furiously inscribing, "I dreamed only of being rid of you . . . I can never trust you again."

In October, Karl disappeared for several days. After his repentant return, the two were reconciled amid loud protestations of love on the part of the uncle. By the summer of 1826, however, Karl was again spending as little time as possible at his uncle's house, and to Beethoven's fury and pain, he received news that his nephew had paid a visit to his mother, Johanna. Beethoven charged the young man with ingratitude in the angriest terms, only to receive more terrifying news still— Karl was threatening to commit suicide because of the overwhelming financial debts he had incurred in the course of his rebellious lifestyle.

Beethoven sent a friend to his nephew at the Institute, but Karl made an excuse to slip away. He went to a pawnbroker and received money for his watch. The money was used to purchase two pistols and ammunition. That night Karl wrote his suicide notes. In the morning, he found a deserted spot and fired both pistols into his head.

Fortunately, Beethoven's nephew apparently did not know how to handle the pistols, or else his intentions were not as authentic as he wished them to appear to be. One shot missed Karl entirely, while the other injured his head only superficially. When he was found, Karl asked to be taken to his mother. A doctor had to be called in, the young man was taken to the hospital, and the matter was reluctantly reported to the police. Beethoven was devastated by every facet of the incident.

Worst yet, when Karl finally agreed to talk about what had happened, he placed the blame on his guardian, saying that Beethoven had imprisoned him with his expectations and tormented him with complaints about his behavior. Nothing was mentioned now about the overwhelming gambling debts that Karl had originally cited as his motive for attempting suicide.

Karl would have his way at last. He would be put into the army. In the meanwhile, the young man returned with Ludwig and his family to recover his health in the country. Again, Beethoven could not control his own worries and suspicions. "You must remember that other people are also human beings," Karl reminded him. "These everlasting unjust reproaches! Why do you make such a disturbance?"

After two months of country living, the family returned to Vienna in December. Beethoven had a miserable return trip in bitter weather which led to his contracting a fever, a severe cough, and a debilitating general weakness. He was very seriously ill. While Beethoven was confined to his bed and attended by doctors, Karl sought to distract him by explaining the multiplication tables to him, writing out examples in one of his conversation books. Beethoven, whose childhood education had been restricted by his father's determination to make a musical prodigy of him, had never advanced as far as multiplication in his knowledge of mathematics.

On January 2, 1827, Karl left for the army. The next day, Beethoven made out his will, leaving everything to his nephew. Beethoven's decline was slow and agonizing, but it was not made in loneliness. Friends and family, gifts and marks of respect visited his sickroom. At first, of course, Beethoven had some hopes of recovery, but he was well aware that he was dying long before that day in March when his friends reported that he said to them, "Friends, applaud; the comedy is over." Later that day, a shipment of special wines arrived. Beethoven looked at them as they sat on the table by his bed. Sadly, he murmured, "Pity, pity—too late!"

For two days the great composer lay unconscious, his heavy breathing rasping at the nerves of those who loved him and waited with him for the end. On the afternoon of March 26, 1827, following a startling clap of thunder and a brilliant flash of lightning from the stormy weather outside, Ludwig van Beethoven opened his eyes. Perhaps even his deaf ears had heard the crashing tones. He stared upward for a moment before his body relaxed. Beethoven had succumbed to cirrhosis of the liver at the age of 56.

At his funeral, before the crowd accompanied his coffin to the grave, a choir intoned his *Miserere*. The spirit of Beethoven breathed through his music. It comforted his friends. It spoke to their hearts—just as it would continue to speak to the hearts of generations.

Conclusion

Ludwig van Beethoven composed thirty-two piano sonatas, sixteen string quartets, nine symphonies, five piano concertos, two Catholic masses, one opera (the *Fidelio*), one ballet *(The Creatures of Prometheus)*, and a stunning multitude of other pieces of music, including folk songs. Some of Beethoven's most famous works include his Fifth and Ninth Symphonies, the *Moonlight Sonata*, and *Fur Elise*.

Beethoven's published works, each assigned an opus number in order of their publication, amount to 138. Some opus numbers, however, refer to more than one piece of music, swelling the count even higher. In addition, there are at least 205 Beethoven compositions without opus numbers and also several unfinished works. The final count gives us 650 known pieces of music that are attributed to the creative genius of Ludwig van Beethoven—that's a lot of opportunities to get to know the soul of Beethoven.

Made in the USA
Middletown, DE
22 September 2022